W9-DAX-569

Favorite Recipes
From Our Kitchen

The
White Gull Inn

DOOR COUNTY

Edited by
Andy Coulson

Printed in the United States of America by
Palmer Publications, Inc.

Copyright © 1990 by Andy and Jan Coulson

All rights reserved.

Reproduction in whole or in part of any portion in any
form without permission is prohibited.

First edition.

Library of Congress Catalog Number: 90-62560

ISBN: 0-942495-06-3

For additional copies of this book, contact:

The White Gull Inn
P.O. Box 159
Fish Creek, Wisconsin 54212

or

Amherst Press
A division of Palmer Publications, Inc.
P.O. Box 296
Amherst, Wisconsin 54406

Contents

Preface

This cookbook, like a candlelight dinner served at the White Gull Inn, is the work of more than one person. Just as the chef, baker, prep cooks, waitresses, and host all contribute to one's ultimate enjoyment of a meal, many of the White Gull staff worked on this project.

We'd like to thank White Gull Baker Steve Glabe, Chef Richard Husbeck, and Kitchen Manager Julie Zak for not only providing recipes, but testing, retesting, and testing again, as the recipes were broken into smaller portions suitable for home cooking. Line Cooks John Vreeke, Dottie Mirkes, Greg Steffen, and John Olson also deserve kudos for their recipe testing, advice and patience. All of the above are responsible for making these recipes turn out—day in and day out, in large quantities and small.

Chefs Kevin McCarty and Michael Halloran are no longer with us, but their many years of creativity in the White Gull kitchen are reflected in this book. We thank them for their recipes and wish them well on their future endeavors.

Thanks to Managers Theresa Ellmann and Laurel Duffin who took this project off the backburner and pushed it to fruition. Theresa's many hours compiling, breaking down, typing, and retyping recipes, followed by evenings testing in her own kitchen, are greatly appreciated. Through her prodding, nudging, cheerleading (and shoving, when necessary!) she kept the rest of us on schedule.

A special thank you to Ann Thorp of the Gibraltar Historical Association who not only provided historical material and old photos, but gave us permission to reprint her excellent account of Dr. Welcker.

Thanks to Master Boiler Russ Ostrand, who for twenty-five years has shared his recipe for the Door County fish boil along with his warm smile and gentle sense of humor. And thanks to all the other White Gull staff, past and present, who have made the White Gull what it is.

Introduction

When we became the White Gull innkeepers in 1972, recipes were kept secret. In fact, we didn't get to see them until after the sale was completed. There were only four of them, and we were instructed not to share them with anyone.

This seemed to make sense at the time. If the inn had only come up with four recipes in 76 years, perhaps they should be kept under lock and key.

Actually, that wasn't the reason. The inn must have had many recipes, secret and otherwise, over the years, but there were only four left in 1972. This was because the inn had ceased serving breakfasts, lunches, and evening meals other than the Door County fish boil. So only four recipes were needed.

Neither Jan nor I had had any formal cooking education. For the first two years, we had our hands full just learning the fish boil and inn business. In our third year, gaining in confidence, we decided to reinstate breakfasts, lunches and the Early American Buffets. The buffets had been introduced by a previous owner, then discontinued before we arrived.

Recipes were not a concern of ours at the time, as I had hired a good cook. However, as cooks go, this one went—two weeks before the season. This was the beginning of Jan's cooking career and both of our interests in recipes. As I learned the challenge of short order cooking (Eggs over-difficult was one of my early specialties), the responsibility of the Early American Buffet fell upon Jan. Pouring over her cookbooks and cooking magazines, she worked out the basic concept. With a certain amount of trepidation, we served our first buffet, and to our surprise and relief, people liked it.

It wasn't long before our recipe files were bursting at the seams. Ideas came from every direction, including our mothers, friends and inn guests. As we could afford to, we hired more staff to help us, and many of them brought recipes and ideas. Even popular dishes had a way of changing and improving as our enthusiastic cooks worked with them. Sometimes necessity was the mother of invention, and new recipes evolved from substitution for an ingredient unavailable in northern Wisconsin on a holiday weekend. More often, fresh local ingredients, like Lake Michigan whitefish, Door County apples and cherries and maple syrup, found their way into our cooking.

Keeping recipes secret didn't make as much sense anymore. A lot of our guests asked for them, and it didn't seem right not to share them. Food editors for newspapers and magazines asked, and we could hardly say no. White Gull recipes began to turn up in some excellent cookbooks, most notably the *Country Inns & Back Roads Cookbook, Best Recipes of Wisconsin Inns and Restaurants* and *The Great American Seafood Cookbook*. Even Chef Tell sent for one to feature on his television show.

The time had come for a change in policy, and our own cookbook seemed in order. We'd like to say the rest was easy, but the real work had just begun. Our talented chefs and cooks rarely work with written recipes, and when they do, the ingredients are in gargantuan amounts, say, to serve 18 or 24 people. Cooking instructions are either non-existent or sketchy, since the recipe's author is usually in our kitchen to explain how it's done. Each recipe had to be broken down to home size quantities, written in language for the lay person, then checked and tested for accuracy.

For years the project progressed in fits and starts, always being pushed to the side when something more pressing occurred. In the restaurant and inn business, something pressing always does occur. It wasn't until we realized this that we decided to make it our number one priority.

Selecting the recipes for inclusion in this book was the easy part. These are the ones most often requested by our guests. We hope you enjoy them.

History of
The White Gull Inn

It could be a story from the 1970's or 1980's: a middle aged professional gives up his lucrative practice and moves to a remote village to become an innkeeper. Except that it happened in 1896.

In the 1890's, Fish Creek, on Wisconsin's Door Peninsula, was a bustling little town that was changing from a fishing community to a summer tourist village. It lacked electricity, telephones, and automobiles; and overland access was limited to a rough and tumble stage ride from Sturgeon Bay. But visitors so appreciated the cool air and peaceful beauty that they were willing to make the trip each summer on the Goodrich Steam Lines from cities around Lake Michigan. One resort, already established, was operated by Asa Thorp, founder of the hamlet.

Enter Dr. Herman Welcker, German born and educated, who at the age of 45, had emigrated to Milwaukee with his wife and daughter. In just two years, Welcker, a virologist, had apparently established an excellent reputation and practice in his adopted city. Then, on a visit to Fish Creek, his life and career would take another twist. Falling in love with the tiny village, Welcker may have realized that if he was going to support his family in Fish Creek, he would have to create a business. He purchased land from Asa Thorp, and constructed what is now the White Gull Inn, naming it after his wife, Henriette.

Welcker surrounded his inn with cottages, and purchased more land around the village, including dock space, a farm to produce food for the inn and property which would later become Welcker's Point in Peninsula State Park. His most unusual project was moving the Lumberman's Hotel from Marinette, Wisconsin, to Fish Creek, in 1907. The hotel (now known as the Whistling Swan) must have been dismantled before being moved the approximately eighteen miles across the frozen waters of Green Bay. Locating his new hotel one block east of the Henriette, Welcker named it Welcker's Casino, because of the card and game tables he provided for men in the basement.

Across the street from the Casino, Dr. Welcker constructed a kitchen

Family portrait of Herman and Henriette Welcker with only daughter, Mathilda.

and dining hall, where all his guests enjoyed three hearty meals a day. He filled his inns and twelve cottages with only the finest of furnishings—walnut dressers with marble tops, oak and iron beds and a baby grand piano, at which Henriette entertained the guests. All had to be shipped in by steamer from cities as far away as Cincinnati.

What was it like to be a guest of Dr. Welcker? Fish Creek historian Ann Thorp, who researched "Herr Doktor," describes him as a "strict disciplinarian, health and fitness enthusiast, gourmet, lover of art, music and nature; vigorous, stubborn, domineering, frugal, snobbish . . . "

"The Doctor presided over his exclusive realm with great pride and a firm hand. An early guest once saw his portly, bearded figure standing on the porch of the Casino, gazing over his resort, and announcing, 'Das ist alles mein!' ('This is all mine!').

"His early guests were often German friends from Milwaukee, people of 'refinement,' perhaps hand-chosen by Welcker. They arrived by steamer, a rigorous trip then, and stayed for the season. The Doctor reserved the right to refuse rooms on whatever basis he chose: attire, personality, or attitude. One story claims that he turned away a young member of the Pabst family and his party because of their racy and outlandish clothes and rather forward manner.

"He designed his program in the manner of European health spas of that era. He believed in exercise, hearty meals, rest, and cultural stimulation. A day's schedule might have begun with a hike along the shore to Ephraim, stopping at one of the little rest areas named for trees in the vicinity; there was a 'Birch Bench,' a 'Balsam Bench,' and others, with water fountains nearby. After returning by boat, perhaps the 'Thistle,' the large noon meal was announced by a big iron bell, and everyone was required to be on time. The table was laden with huge platters of roast pork or Wiener Schnitzel, potatoes, noodles, baked cabbage, and other vegetables, smoked fish, fresh bread, and rich desserts such as a three-layer cherry kuchen liberally crowned with whipped cream.

"A two-hour 'silent' period followed and was strictly enforced. Herr Doktor strode through cottages and hallways shaking a small hand bell, calling 'Ruhe, Ruhe!' ('Quiet, quiet!')

"Swimming was a favorite pastime and exercise for the Doctor and his wife Henriette, and guests were encouraged to join them for an afternoon dip at the Bathing Beach (now the Town Beach). Bathing costumes were made of dark wool; a two-piece suit for men, knee length (one rather imperious man was seen entering the water with his Phi Beta Kappa pin fastened to his bathing suit). Women wore voluminous skirts and bloomers and often a white hat pinned to their hair, creating a merry picture of white dots floating and bobbing on the water.

"After another hearty meal the evenings were devoted to music, games, and socializing at the Casino. Women had a sewing room and a card room for bridge or Mah Jong. Game and billiard tables were set up in the basement for the men, and there were ping-pong tables and other amusements for children. There were ice boxes stocked with beer and other beverages, available on an honor system.

Summer visitors arriving by steamers, circa 1910.

Dr. Herman Welcker and Henriette Welcker, founders of the White Gull Inn, enjoying an afternoon dip at the Fish Creek bathing beach.

In 1913, guests at Welcker's Resort posed for a group photo on the porch of the Casino.

Harbor View, Fish Creek, Wis.

An early view of Fish Creek and the harbor.

"Plays were presented starring some of the guests or visiting actors, and concerts performed by professional musicians from Chicago and Milwaukee. The great opera singer Madame Schumann-Heinck once sang at the Casino. The great hall was hung with paintings by famous artists. Guests sometimes went to the Town Hall to see the flickery movies of that time.

"At ten o'clock sharp the day was over and all the kerosene lamps were to be extinguished. Herr Doktor patrolled the walks and would shout up to a lighted window, 'Abdrehen!' ('Turn it off!').

"Welcker had his office in his home, across from the Casino. Guests went there to pay their weekly bill and were amazed at his collection of snake skins, butterflies, antlers, a boar's head, stuffed fish, and stacks of books and sheet music.

"Evidently he gave up his medical practice when he established his resort, but he would occasionally prescribe for a mild illness. He had once studied virology, and when a smallpox epidemic threatened the village, he undertook the task of manufacturing a vaccine. At the time he didn't have the breed of cattle necessary for the production of the vaccine. Instead, he used a local boy, Merle Thorp, then about eleven years old. Merle was vaccinated over and over, and the Doctor used his blood to make vaccine for the rest of 'der kinder' in the town.

Dr. Welcker, arm in arm with two young ladies, on a boat trip from Fish Creek to Chambers Island.

"Throughout the warm summer days the figure of Herr Doktor prevailed, a sometimes romantic image. There is an old photo of him, on a boat trip to Chambers Island, with a lovely young lady on each arm, his bright eyes showing his pleasure and admiration. His old-world sentimentality was evident when he named the cottages for the women in his life—the Henriette, the Matilda, the Hermine, the Tina, the Minna, and the Else."

After Henriette's death in 1920 and Herman's in 1924, Welcker's Resort was managed by a niece, Martha Fahr, until her death in 1939. Then Welcker's domain was split up, with his inns and other properties going to various owners.

The Henriette went through a succession of owners and several name changes, including Sunset Park Guest Home

The White Gull Inn as it looked in the 1940's. At that time, it was known as Sunset Park Guest House.

and Lakewood Lodge. During the 1950's and 1960's, many of Door County's classic old inns were either torn down or remodeled beyond recognition to accommodate the public's changing tastes in travel. Perhaps the Henriette would eventually have suffered the same fate had it not been purchased, in 1959, by a young couple from Madison.

Andy Redmann was a talented artist who could see beyond the aging facade. He and his wife, Elsie, changed the name to the White Gull Inn and set out to create their version of a New England style hostelry. The Redmanns refinished the pine floors on the second floor, papered the walls with colorful prints, refinished much of the original furniture and acquired more turn-of-the-century furniture. Andy's watercolors were featured throughout the inn and cottages.

Andy turned his attention to the 1940's era dining room, which had been added after Welcker's Resort had been split up. A warm, Early American look emerged with the addition of the two-way fireplace, wainscotted walls, small paned windows and rough-sawn hemlock ceiling. As resourceful as he was artistic, Andy fashioned the colonial-style chandeliers out of funnels, copper tubing, and muffin tins, soldered together and spray-painted black.

Elsie took over the kitchen, where for most of the year she did all the cooking and baking by herself. One of her creations was the Early American Buffet, which consisted of roast turkey and ham, baked beans, corn bread, and home-made butter, churned by the young staff in the dining room.

The most popular meal started by the Redmanns, and one the inn is still known for today, is the traditional Door County fish boil. Until the 1950's, the meal, consisting of boiled fresh whitefish or lake trout, boiled red potatoes, rye bread, and cherry pie, had enjoyed popularity in backyard and church picnics, but had not been discovered by the general public. In back of the inn, in the shade of the century old maple trees, Andy created a flagstone patio surrounded by a cedar hedge. Tables and chairs were set up for guests to watch the catch of the day prepared before them over an open fire. Andy boiled the fish, Elsie prepared the breads and pies, and an accordian player would entertain the guests before and during their meal. That first year, the fish boil was held one night a week. Today, the fish boil is served four evenings a week, and guests make reservations weeks ahead, especially in summer.

The Redmanns owned the inn for five years. Afterwards they bought an old cherry orchard on the Fish Creek bluff, where they eventually established the Settlement Courtyard Inn and Shop Complex.

Jan and I have been the innkeepers at the White Gull since 1972, a tenure longer than anyone other than the Welckers. Our arrival was exciting, hectic, somewhat disorganized, and I am convinced we didn't really know what we were doing.

After graduating from the University of Wisconsin in 1968, I had worked as a reporter for 18 months before deciding to emigrate to Australia. A year and a half later, after working my way around that country, I found myself living in Perisher Valley up in the Snowy Mountains, employed as a surveyor's assistant. I liked Australia and might still be there today, had I not received a telegram from an old college friend in May of 1972. The White Gull Inn was for sale. Would I join him and three other friends in buying it? A week later, I was in Fish Creek, learning the business and trying to ready the inn for a Memorial Day weekend opening. My bartending experience in Australia was apparently enough for my partners, as I was voted manager.

With more than a little help from our friends, my partners and I managed to clean the rooms and cottages, hire a staff, and open on time. We were lucky to be as young and as inexperienced as we were, or we might never have had the courage to proceed. In 1972, Americans outside of New England had never heard of country inns, and bed and breakfast was a concept most people identified with Europe. The White Gull was a relic of a bygone era at a time when new motels and condominiums were the norm.

One of the first people I hired was 18-year-old Jan Lindsley, who had just graduated from high school in Green Bay, and moved to Door County. Growing up in a family as one of nine children probably prepared Jan for her future in innkeeping as much as anything.

Those early years were hard work, but a lot of fun too. We tried to make up for our lack of capital and experience with enthusiasm, and somehow, what began as a lark became a labor of love. We decided to restore rather than replace and look for customers who shared our love of tradition.

An innkeeper must be able to wear many hats, and in the early years, Jan worked in nearly every position at the inn, including housekeeping, waitressing, hostessing, cooking, and baking. I was usually at the front desk, but when I had a chance, I'd be out on the patio helping Russ Ostrand boil the fish and sometimes accompanying his accordian playing with my five-string banjo. Jan and I were married in 1975.

By the time we arrived, the White Gull kitchen had fallen into disrepair, and the only meal remaining was the fish boil. As soon as we could, we revived the breakfasts, lunches, and the popular Early American Buffet. (One of Jan's recipes for the Early American Buffet, Corn and Clam Pie, is included in this book.) Eventually we changed the buffets to the Candlelight Dinners, which are now served on the evenings when there is not a fish boil.

It seemed as though the main building and cottages were under a never-ending remodeling and redecorating schedule. Eventually, all received new foundations, plumbing, wiring, and were fully insulated for winter use. Jan redecorated the rooms and cottages with coordinating prints and fabrics, utilizing many of the original antiques as well as others we've collected.

Slowly, our clientele began to grow, and our season grew from three months to six. In 1977, a man named Norman Simpson came to visit. He was the author of a book called *Country Inns and Back Roads,* and according to him, there were other inns like ours out there, and a growing number of people who liked to visit them. We happily accepted his invitation to be in his book, and since then, have watched the country inn movement sweep the country.

The years have flown by. We've managed to expand the dining room, add two more cottages and a staff house. After becoming the sole owners in the early 1980's, we purchased a large home about a block from the inn. Built by the first grocer of Fish Creek, the Lundberg House is now a four-bedroom guest house for the inn.

In 1985, our interest in historic Fish Creek led us to purchase the original Welcker's Casino building. The Casino had also undergone a succession of different names and owners after Dr. Welcker's death. Reunited with its sister inn, the Whistling Swan has now been totally renovated and reopened as a seven-room Bed and Breakfast inn. It is also the home of Jan's Whistling Swan Shop.

Today, I'm still at the White Gull, while Jan holds fort at the Whistling Swan. When we're not innkeeping, we retreat to our old farm outside of Fish Creek with our three daughters, Meredith, Emilie, and Hannah.

By now, innkeeping is in our blood and it is hard to imagine being anything but the keepers of the White Gull. After all, where else would we both get to wear the hats of cook, hotelier, decorator, restorer, landscaper, housekeeper, maintenance person, fish boiler (the list never ends!) all in the same day? We've had a lot of fun, made hundreds of friends and have enough wonderful memories to last a lifetime.

Jan and Andy Coulson, innkeepers.

The White Gull Inn

Est. 1896

Breakfast

Notes

Gingerbread Pancakes

1¼ cups flour
3 tablespoons sugar
1 tablespoon baking powder
1½ teaspoons baking soda
½ teaspoon salt
2 eggs
1 teaspoon dry ground ginger
1 cup buttermilk
2 tablespoons melted butter
½ cup molasses

Combine dry ingredients in a bowl. In separate bowl, mix eggs and buttermilk. Pour eggs and buttermilk into dry ingredients and stir until smooth. Add melted butter and molasses to batter and stir to combine.

Cook on hot griddle lightly coated with vegetable oil. Flip pancakes when bubbles appear on surface, and bottom side is well browned. Serve with Door County Maple Syrup. Yield: 12 medium sized (4″ diameter) pancakes.

White Gull Buttermilk Pancakes

1 cup flour
3 tablespoons sugar
1 tablespoon baking powder
1½ teaspoons baking soda
¼ teaspoon salt
2 eggs
1¼ cups buttermilk
2½ tablespoons melted butter

Combine dry ingredients in a bowl. In a separate bowl, mix eggs and buttermilk. Pour eggs and buttermilk into dry ingredients and stir until smooth. Add melted butter to batter.

Cook on hot griddle lightly coated with vegetable oil. Filp pancakes when bubbles appear on surface and bottom side is golden brown. Serve with butter and Door County maple syrup. Yield: 10-12, 4-5" pancakes.

For Door County cherry or apple pancakes, drop cherries or thin slices of apples onto pancakes right before flipping.

Johnnycakes

3 cups cornmeal
½ cup flour
⅔ teaspoon baking soda
1 tablespoon sugar
1½ teaspoons salt
4 eggs
3 cups buttermilk
1 tablespoon melted butter

Separate eggs and beat the egg whites until stiff, set aside. Combine dry ingredients in a bowl. In separate bowl mix egg yolks and buttermilk thoroughly, then pour into the dry ingredients and stir until smooth. Add melted butter to the batter. Fold stiffly beaten egg whites into the batter gently.

Cook on hot griddle lightly coated with vegetable oil. Flip pancakes when bubbles appear on surface and bottom side is golden brown. Serve with butter and Door County maple syrup. Yield: 12 large pancakes.

Oatmeal Pancakes

1 cup flour
2 teaspoons baking powder
½ teaspoon salt
2 eggs
½ can evaporated milk
⅓ cup cold water
¼ cup melted butter
2½ cups cooked oatmeal

Combine dry ingredients. Add eggs, milk, water, and butter. Blend in cooked oatmeal.

Cook on hot griddle lightly coated with vegetable oil. Flip pancakes when bubbles appear on surface, and bottom side is golden brown. Serve with butter and Door County Maple Syrup. Yield: 6 to 8 medium sized pancakes.

Buckwheat Pancakes

1 cup buckwheat flour
1 cup all-purpose flour
2 tablespoons baking powder
1 tablespoon baking soda
2 teaspoons sugar
1 teaspoon salt
3 eggs, separated
1 quart buttermilk
¼ cup melted butter

In separate bowl, beat egg whites until stiff. Set aside. In another bowl, combine all dry ingredients. Add yolks, butter, and buttermilk, and stir until well combined. Slowly fold in beaten whites.

Cook on hot griddle lightly coated with vegetable oil. Flip pancakes when bubbles appear on surface, and bottom side is golden brown. Serve with butter and Door County maple syrup. Yield: 12 large pancakes.

Breakfast

Broccoli Omelette

1 tablespoon butter
½ cup diced onions
½ cup diced mushrooms
½ bunch of chopped broccoli (separate tips from stems)
½ teaspoon marjoram
1 teaspoon garlic
½ teaspoon thyme
½ teaspoon pepper
1 tablespoon flour
½ cup cream

Saute broccoli stems, onions, mushrooms, and seasonings in butter until vegetables are tender. Add broccoli tips and cook 3 munutes. Add flour and cook approximately 10 additional minutes. Finish by adding ½ cup cream to broccoli mixture. Stir and cook for an additional 2 minutes. When preparing finished omelette, filling should be spooned onto eggs when they become 'set' in the frypan. At this time cheese may also be placed over the filling, and the omelette folded over upon itself for the final cooking period. Serve immediately. Yield: Enough filling for two generously filled, or three modestly filled omelettes.

Hollandaise Sauce

3 egg yolks
Juice of one lemon
2 tablespoons very hot melted butter

Whip egg yolks and lemon juice at high speed in blender until very smooth and bright yellow. Add very hot butter slowly into blender while on high speed until mixture thickens. Serve immediately. Makes ½ cup, or enough for two servings of Eggs Benedict.

Blueberry Coffee Cake

2 cups fresh or frozen blueberries
½ cup butter
¾ cup sugar
3 eggs
1 cup sour cream
2 cups flour
1½ teaspoons baking powder
1 teaspoon baking soda
1 teaspoon vanilla extract

TOPPING:
1½ cups brown sugar
2 tablespoons cinnamon
¾ cup chopped nuts of your choice

Mix sour cream and baking soda together in a small bowl and set aside to react. Cream butter and sugar together. Add eggs. Add flour, baking powder, and vanilla. Pour foamy sour cream mixture into batter and mix well.

Spread one half of mixture in greased 9"x13" pan. Sprinkle blueberries over this base layer, then sprinkle ⅓ of the crumb topping over the blueberries. Spread the other half of the batter into the pan, then sprinkle the remaining topping over the cake. Bake at 325 degrees for one hour or until toothpick or knife inserted comes out clean.

Corned Beef Hash

2 cups coarsely shredded, precooked corned beef brisket
4 baked potatoes, cooled, peeled, and grated
½ cup grated onion
¼ pound butter

   Mix together all ingredients except butter. Melt butter in hot skillet. Add hash, and fry at least 5 minutes on the first side. Divide the hash into four servings with spatula and turn to brown again for 5 to 7 minutes on the second side. If desired, crack an egg over each serving and cover skillet with tight fitting lid 3 minutes before serving, (four minutes may be necessary for obtaining firmer yolks). Serve hot and crispy from the frying pan. Serves four.

White Gull Granola

1 cup rolled wheat flakes
1 cup shredded coconut
1 cup chopped walnuts or mixed nuts
½ cup sunflower seeds
⅓ cup sesame seeds
8 cups rolled oats
⅓ cup water
¾ cup honey
½ teaspoon vanilla
1 cup wheat germ
¾ cup vegetable oil
2 cups raisins

Mix together all dry ingredients in large bowl. In separate small bowl, mix together water, vanilla, oil, and honey until well blended. Stir wet ingredients slowly into dry, to evenly distribute throughout mixture. Spread granola mixture out onto two large cookie sheets, and bake at 300 degrees for 45 minutes, turning granola with a pancake turner every 15 minutes and browning evenly. Leave granola spread out on baking sheets to completely cool, at least 2 hours. When completely cooled, stir in raisins, and place in airtight storage container. Yield: Approximately 15 cups.

Cherry Stuffed French Toast

1 8-oz. package cream cheese, at room temperature
1 cup red tart Door County cherries, drained
1 loaf unsliced egg bread
6 eggs, well beaten
¹/₃ cup heavy cream
cinnamon

Slice the egg bread into 1½″ slices. Cut each slice down ¾ of its length so that you have almost formed two slices of bread, but the bottom ¼ still holds the entire piece together. Set aside.

Beat cream cheese, heavy cream, and cherries together on medium speed until well combined.

Spread approximately ¼ cup of the mixture into the pocket of each slice, and press the slice together very gently, distributing the filling evenly.

Dip each slice of the stuffed egg bread lightly into the beaten egg mixture to coat all sides. Place immediately onto a lightly oiled griddle. Sprinkle lightly with cinnamon and turn when golden brown. After frying the second side until golden, remove each slice to a cutting board, and very gently slice each piece in half diagonally. To garnish, sprinkle with powdered sugar. Arrange the triangles on plates and serve immediately with Door County maple syrup. Yield: 4 servings

Breakfast

25

The
White Gull Inn
Est. 1896

Breads

Notes

Lemon Bread

1¼ cups sugar
½ cup vegetable oil
4 teaspoons lemon rind
2 teaspoons lemon extract
2 eggs
2 cups flour
½ teaspoon salt
3½ teaspoons baking powder
¾ cup milk

Cream together sugar, shortening, lemon flavorings, and beat in the eggs. In separate bowl, sift together flour, salt and baking powder. Add dry ingredients and milk to creamed mixture. Grease loaf pans. Bake small loaves for about 45 minutes at 350 degrees, or until knife inserted comes out clean. The large loaf will take 60 to 65 minutes. Remove from pans to cool on rack.

Makes one large (8"x4") loaf, or 3 small (5¾"x3") loaves.

Breads

Blueberry Bread

1¼ cups sugar
½ cup vegetable oil
2 eggs
1¾ cups flour
½ teaspoon salt
½ teaspoon baking powder
⅔ cup milk
1 cup blueberries

Cream sugar and shortening together until smooth. Add eggs, flour, salt, baking powder, and milk. Beat until smooth. Fold in blueberries slowly until well distributed.

Grease loaf pans and fill half full with batter. Bake at 300 degrees for 50 to 60 minutes for one large loaf (8"x4"), or 30 to 40 minutes for the 3 small loaves (5¾"x3").

Cranberry Bread

2 cups flour
1 cup sugar
1 teaspoon baking powder
½ teaspoon baking soda
1 teaspoon salt
¼ cup butter
2 eggs
¾ cup orange juice
1 teaspoon orange peel
1 cup coarsely chopped cranberries
½ cup chopped nuts

Combine flour, sugar, baking soda, baking powder, and salt in mixing bowl. Cut in butter with fork or pastry blender, or on medium speed of electric mixer. Add eggs, juice, and peel. Mix until well combined. Stir in cranberries and nuts by hand until evenly distributed throughout batter.

Bake in greased bread tins at 350 degrees. Batter will make one large 8"x4" loaf, or two 5¾"x3" mini loaves. Mini loaves will need 45 to 50 minutes baking time, the large loaf 60 to 65 minutes.

Breads

Carrot Bread

¾ cup sugar
2 eggs
½ cup vegetable oil
1 teaspoon vanilla
1½ cups flour
½ teaspoon salt
2 teaspoons baking soda
¼ teaspoon cinnamon
1½ cups carrots, grated
1 cup walnuts

Combine sugar, eggs, oil, and vanilla in mixing bowl and beat on medium speed until well blended. Add flour, salt, soda, and cinnamon and mix one minute more. Add carrots and walnuts and stir until thoroughly combined.

Pour batter into one greased 8″x4″ loaf pan or two 5¾″x3″ mini loaf pans. Bake at 350 degrees. Mini loaves will need 45 to 50 minutes, the large loaf 60 to 65 minutes.

Spicy Apple Bread

½ cup vegetable oil
¾ cup brown sugar, firmly packed
2 eggs
½ cup buttermilk
1 teaspoon vanilla
2¼ cups flour
1 teaspoon baking soda
1 teaspoon salt
½ teaspoon nutmeg
1 teaspoon cinnamon
¼ teaspoon ground cloves
1 cup chopped apples, NOT peeled, but cored

Cream the shortening, sugar, and eggs. Add the buttermilk and vanilla and mix until very smooth. Add other dry ingredients gradually, mixing well. Fold apples and nuts into batter last of all.

Bake at 350 degrees in well greased pans. This recipe will make one 8"x4" size loaf, or two 5¾"x3" mini loaves. The large loaf will require 60 to 65 minutes of baking time, and the mini loaves will require 45 to 50 minutes.

Breads

Orange Date Nut Bread

1 cup dates
½ cup water
¼ cup butter
1 egg
1 cup sugar
2 cups flour
1 teaspoon baking powder
1 teaspoon salt
1 teaspoon baking soda
½ cup chopped nuts
1 orange

Grate the entire rind of one orange, and set aside. Puree remaining fruit of the orange and set aside in mixing bowl. Cook dates, water, and butter over medium heat until dates are softened completely.

Combine the simmered date mixture and blended orange in mixing bowl and blend thoroughly. Stir in grated orange peel. Add remaining dry ingredients gradually blending well.

Grease bread loaf pans and fill ½ with batter. This recipe will make one large 8″x4″ loaf, or two smaller 5¾″x3″ mini loaves. Baking time for large loaf is 60 to 65 minutes, for the mini loaves 45 to 50 minutes. Bake at 350 degrees.

Pumpkin Nut Bread

2½ cups sugar
1¼ cups milk
1 cup canned pumpkin
3 eggs
⅓ cup vegetable oil
3¼ cups all-purpose flour
1 teaspoon salt
1 teaspoon baking powder
1 teaspoon baking soda
1 teaspoon cinnamon
½ teaspoon cloves
½ teaspoon ginger
½ teaspoon nutmeg
¾ cup coarsely chopped nuts

Combine sugar, milk, eggs, pumpkin, and oil in large mixing bowl. Combine flour, salt, baking powder, baking soda, and spices; stir into pumpkin mixture until well blended. Fold in walnuts.

Pour batter evenly into 4 greased 5¾"x3" loaf pans or 2 greased 8"x4" loaf pans. Bake in preheated 350-degree oven 45 to 50 minutes for mini loaves and 60 to 70 minutes for large loaves. Cool in pans 10 minutes. Remove and cool completely on wire rack.

Breads

35

Steve's Limpa Bread

rind of one orange, grated
1½ cups buttermilk
1 cup brown sugar, firmly packed
¼ cup molasses
1½ tablespoons caraway seed
1½ teaspoons salt
1½ teaspoons anise seed
1 cup water
2 1-oz. packages dry yeast
¾ cup warm water (95-100 degrees)
2 eggs
7 cups white flour, sifted
2 cups rye flour

In a medium saucepan, heat orange rind, buttermilk, brown sugar, molasses, caraway seed, salt, anise seed, and the 1 cup water until warmed, and brown sugar is dissolved. Set aside.

In a small mixing bowl, combine yeast, the ¾ cup warm water, and eggs. Mix thoroughly and let sit until yeast is fully dissolved.

In a large mixing bowl, place 3 of the 7 cups of white flour and stir in the yeast mixture. Add ½ of the buttermilk mixture and stir well. Add rye flour and stir again. Add the rest of the buttermilk mixture and stir to blend. Add the final 4 cups of white flour and knead for 5 minutes until dough is smooth and any lumps are worked out. Place in greased bowl, cover with a kitchen cloth or plastic wrap, and set in a warm place until dough is doubled in size, (about one hour). Punch down dough at this point and divide into 3 equal parts. Shape into loaves. Place into greased bread loaf pans and allow to rise again until doubled (approximately one hour).

Bake in 325-degree oven for 35 to 40 minutes. Remove from pans and cool completely on rack before slicing. Yield: 3 standard size loaves.

The
White Gull Inn
Est. 1896

Soups

Notes

Carrot Soup

2 tablespoons butter
1 medium onion, thinly sliced
4 large carrots, peeled and thinly sliced
1 quart chicken stock
1 teaspoon salt
pepper to taste
1 cup whipping cream

Heat butter in saucepan and simmer onions three minutes. Add carrots and simmer three minutes more. Add stock and salt and simmer 20 minutes. Remove from heat and allow to cool.

Process in food processor or blender thoroughly until mixture becomes a very fine puree. Strain through a fine to medium sieve. Return soup to saucepan, bring to a boil, and reduce heat. Add cream. Do not allow to boil again once cream has been added.

If you desire a thicker soup, add 1 to 2 tablespoons flour to a small amount of prepared soup, and mix with a whisk until very smooth. Then return flour mixture to simmering soup slowly, stirring constantly, and continue to cook for at least one minute more.

NOTE: When straining soup, at least $1/3$ of initial volume will be removed by the sieve. Discard this vegetable residue. Garnish with croutons and parsley. Yield: 4 servings.

Cheesey Cauliflower Soup

1 head cauliflower, finely chopped
1 medium onion, finely chopped
2 stalks celery, finely chopped
1 cup flour
1 cup butter
8 cups chicken broth
1 pint cream
1½ cups medium to sharp cheddar cheese, finely shredded
salt and pepper to taste

Melt butter and add celery and onions. Saute until slightly tender. Add flour and stir. Cook 5 minutes. Add chicken broth and cauliflower and simmer 30 minutes. Add cream, cheese, salt, and pepper. Reduce heat to simmer and cook 10 minutes more, stirring often. Yield: Approximately 1 gallon.

Shrimp Bisque

1 large onion, chopped
4 stalks celery, chopped
⅛ pound butter
1 pound shrimp, raw
1 cup heavy cream
2 bay leaves
1 teaspoon white pepper
½ teaspoon Tabasco sauce

Boil shrimp in ¾ gallon water for 8 minutes. Drain shrimp and reserve water (stock). Saute onion and celery in butter until onions are transparent. Add ½ gallon of shrimp stock. Simmer. Add shrimp and stir. Thicken with roux. (See below.)

ROUX: Melt ⅓ cup of butter in small, heavy saucepan. Slowly mix in ⅓ cup flour and continue mixing over medium heat for one minute.

Add cream, bay leaves, pepper, and Tabasco. Continue to simmer 30 more minutes. Pour into blender or food processor, and puree thoroughly. (Remove bay leaves before pureeing.) Return to heat and bring almost to a boil. Serve immediately. Serves: 8 to 10.

41

Cream of Broccoli Soup

1 bunch broccoli, finely chopped
1 medium onion, finely chopped
2 stalks celery, finely chopped
1 cup butter
1 cup flour
8 cups chicken broth
¼ teaspoon black pepper
¼ teaspoon salt
1 pint cream

Melt butter and add celery and onion. Cook until slightly tender. Add flour and cook 5 minutes, stirring frequently. Add chicken broth and broccoli and simmer 30 minutes. Add cream and salt and pepper. Reduce heat to simmer and cook 10 minutes more, stirring often.

NOTE: Whole milk can also be used in place of cream, but be very careful not to boil the soup after adding the milk, so the soup does not curdle. Yield: Approximately 1 gallon.

Potato-Cucumber Soup

6 potatoes, peeled and cubed
2 cucumbers, peeled and chopped
1 medium onion, chopped
2 stalks celery, chopped
1 cup butter
1 cup flour
2 tablespoons dill weed
8 cups chicken broth
1 pint cream
1 cup sour cream

Melt butter. Saute onion and celery until tender. Add flour and cook 5 minutes, stirring constantly. Add potatoes, cucumbers, dill, and chicken broth. Boil until potatoes are cooked. Cool slightly and puree in a blender. Add cream and sour cream. Reheat to near, but not quite boiling, and serve. Yield: Approximately 12 cups.

Chicken Almond Soup

1 cup celery, chopped
2 cups mushrooms, chopped
1 cup onion, chopped
1 quart chicken stock
white pepper to taste
2 cups chicken, cooked and boned
2 tablespoons almond extract
chicken fat or butter roux
cream or milk

Saute celery, onion, and mushrooms in butter. Add the chicken stock, chicken, white pepper, and almond extract. Thicken with roux.

ROUX: Melt ¼ cup butter over medium heat. Whisk in ¼ cup flour and blend until smooth. Cook another minute over medium heat, stirring constantly.

Add cream or milk to bring to desired consistency. Garnish with slivered almonds sprinkled over each serving. Yield: Approximately 2 quarts.

Seafood Bisque

4 cups raw shrimp with shells
2 cups water
2 cups diced onions
2 cups diced celery
1 cup butter
1 cup flour
½ teaspoon nutmeg
1½ teaspoons tarragon
1 wedge lemon
2 teaspoons minced parsley
½ teaspoon each salt and pepper
2 bay leaves
4 cups fish stock (or substitute 1 tablespoon seafood base
   to 1 cup water)
1 cup water (from shrimp)
4 tablespoons white wine
1 quart heavy cream
1 cup sour cream
4 cups chopped clams

Simmer shrimp in water. Drain, reserving water. Cool shrimp, shell and devein. Simmer water, reducing it to 1 cup. Melt butter in heavy soup pot or dutch oven. Add onion, celery, and saute for 2 minutes. Add flour, and stir to blend thoroughly. Cook on low heat for 5 minutes. Add salt, pepper, bay leaves, tarragon, nutmeg, lemon wedge, and parsley. Stir for 2 minutes.

Add water from shrimp, fish stock, and wine. Simmer over low heat till thickened. Add shrimp, clams, and simmer 5 minutes. Add cream. Warm (do not boil). Serve. Yield: Makes 3½ quarts.

Soups

Rich's Clam Chowder

2 tablespoons butter
½ cup diced celery
½ cup onions
½ cup carrots
1 cup tomatoes, seeded
1 pound raw clams
2 ounces cream Sherry
4 cups clam stock
1 quart heavy cream
½ teaspoon salt
¼ teaspoon white pepper

ROUX:
⅓ cup melted butter
⅓ cup flour

Melt butter in large, heavy, deep saucepan. Saute onions, celery, carrots 3 to 4 minutes. Add cream Sherry and Clams. Cook 3 to 4 minutes. Add tomatoes and stock. Bring to boil and simmer 10 minutes. Add cream.

To make roux: melt ⅓ cup of butter in small shallow saucepan. Slowly mix in ⅓ cup flour and continue mixing over medium heat for one minute.

Thicken the chowder with freshly prepared roux and simmer for 20 minutes more. Yield: 2 quarts.

Whitefish Chowder

½ pound raw diced bacon
2 cups diced raw onions
2 pounds whitefish, deboned, cut into 1-inch pieces
6 large potatoes, pared and cubed
1 large can (51 oz.) chicken broth
6 cups half and half
1 teaspoon salt
½ teaspoon white pepper

Saute bacon until all fat is cooked out. Remove bacon from pan and fry onion in remaining fat, saute 5 minutes. Add potatoes and stock. Simmer for 5 minutes. Then add the whitefish and cook until potatoes are tender. Add cream and season to taste. Be careful not to boil after cream is added. Add bacon bits during final simmering. Yield: Approximately 1 gallon.

Soups

The
White Gull Inn
Est. 1896

Salads

Notes

White Gull Potato Salad

1¼ cups sour cream
½ cup vegetable oil
3 eggs at room temperature
½ cup Dijon mustard
5 teaspoons dill, dried
1 tablespoon red wine vinegar
1 tablespoon lemon juice, fresh
1 tablespoon salt
1 tablespoon sugar
½ teaspoon pepper
1 medium onion, chopped
½ bunch celery stalks, chopped
5 pounds small red potatoes, unpeeled

Blend eggs, mustard, dill, vinegar, lemon juice, salt, sugar, and pepper on medium high speed of electric blender until slightly thickened. Gradually add oil with machine running and continue to blend for 30 seconds more. Pour into large bowl and stir in sour cream until well blended. Set aside to chill.

Cook potatoes in salted water until just done (slightly crunchy). Do not overcook. Slice, but do not peel potatoes, and mix together with celery and onion.

Mix vegetables together with dressing until well incorporated. Chill for 30 minutes and serve. Yield: 14 cups.

Smoked Turkey, Apple, and Walnut Salad

2 cups smoked turkey, chunked
3 Granny Smith, or other tart apples, cored and diced
1½ cups celery, chopped
1 cup parsley, chopped
1 cup citrus mustard dressing (found below)
1 cup chopped toasted walnuts

Toss turkey, apples, celery and chopped parsley. Blend in dressing. Cover and refrigerate. Sprinkle with nuts when serving. Yield: Approximately four servings.

Citrus Mustard Dressing

1 tablespoon fresh orange juice
4 teaspoons Dijon mustard
1 egg yolk
¼ teaspoon salt
¼ teaspoon finely ground pepper
1 teaspoon honey
1 cup olive oil
1 tablespoon lemon juice

Combine orange juice, mustard, egg yolk, salt, pepper, and honey on medium speed in blender. Slowly add olive oil in steady stream while blender is operating on low speed, until dressing is thickened. Add lemon juice and blend slowly again for 10 seconds until thoroughly mixed. Yield: 1½ cups.

Chicken Waldorf Salad

2 cups mayonaise
¼ cup sour cream
2 tablespoons honey
2 cups diced celery
4 cups cored and chunked apples
2 cups raisins
3½ cups diced cooked chicken
2 cups walnuts, (added as served!)

Mix together until well blended: mayonnaise, sour cream, and honey. Combine other ingredients and toss with dressing. Add walnuts just prior to serving. Serve on a bed of lettuce greens. Yield: Six servings.

Salads

Pasta Salad

¼ head broccoli, cut into bite-sized pieces
¼ head cauliflower, cut into bite-sized pieces
4 green onions, chopped
4 stalks celery, chopped
1 cup black olives, sliced
½ cup tomato, fresh and sliced, or 10 cherry tomatoes
½ cup carrots, julienne sliced
1½ cups uncooked corkscrew pasta

Boil pasta until cooked al dente and rinse well. Add cooked pasta and 1½ cups of the White Gull Inn Italian salad dressing found on page 63, to vegetables and toss to mix well. Let stand, refrigerated, 6 to 8 hours to marinate. Yield: 12 cups.

Chicken Tenders Salad

4 skinned and boneless chicken breast halves,
cut into one-inch strips.
½ cup milk
1 cup flour
3 tablespoons sesame seeds
1 tablespoon onion salt
1 tablespoon garlic powder
1 teaspoon paprika
½ teaspoon black pepper
1 teaspoon salt
½ teaspoon cayenne pepper
1 quart deep frying oil
salad ingredients (see below)

Mix all dry ingredients, (flour, seeds, and spices) together in shallow bowl or pie pan. Dip chicken pieces completely into milk, then dredge through seasoned flour to coat well. Fry immediately in hot deep frying oil until golden brown and delicately crisp; approximately 3 to 5 minutes. Drain on paper toweling. Meanwhile, arrange on 4 individual salad plates, fresh mixed garden greens for base, such as Romaine, Boston Bib, Iceberg, Butterhead lettuce, or fresh spinach, torn into bite-sized pieces.

Then arrange next, in layers as you desire; rings of Bermuda onion, cherry tomatoes, hard boiled egg wedges, alfalfa sprouts, green pepper rings, radish slices, etc . . .

Place chicken strips over all to complete the individual salads.

Our most complimentary dressing for the chicken tenders salad is the Creamy Cracked Peppercorn dressing found on page 60. Yield: 4 servings.

Salads

White Gull Coleslaw

6 cups grated cabbage
1 cup grated carrots
¼ cup grated celery
¼ cup grated radishes
2 tablespoons onion, grated

Slaw Sauce

¾ teaspoon celery salt
¾ teaspoon caraway seed
1 tablespoon vinegar
2 tablespoons sugar
1 cup "Miracle Whip"-type salad dressing

Mix slaw sauce together first, and stir until smooth and well blended. Just prior to serving, pour slaw sauce over vegetables, and stir well to combine. Serve well chilled. Yield: 8 cups.

The
White Gull Inn
Est. 1896

Salad Dressings

Notes

Curried Poppy Seed Dressing

1½ cups honey
1½ teaspoons salt
¾ cup vinegar
2 cups salad oil
¼ cup red onion, grated
2 teaspoons curry powder
1 tablespoon poppy seeds

Combine all ingredients in electric mixer, food processor, or blender and blend on slow to medium speed for at least one minute until smooth and thoroughly blended. Yield: 4½ cups.

Hot Bacon Dressing

1 pound bacon, diced
1 small onion, diced
1 teaspoon dry mustard
1 teaspoon freshly ground pepper
1 tablespoon chopped fresh parsley
1½ cups water
¾ cup cider vinegar
½ cup brown sugar
1 tablespoon corn starch

Fry bacon until very crisp. Drain well. Add onion, mustard, pepper, parsley, water, and brown sugar. Mix vinegar and cornstarch together until smooth and free of lumps, and add slowly to the other mixed ingredients. Bring to a boil, stirring constantly, cook for one more minute. Remove from heat, and prepare greens for salad. Serve warm over tossed greens. Yield: 3 cups.

Creamy Cracked Peppercorn

3¹⁄₃ cups sour cream
½ cup buttermilk
2 tablespoons cracked pepper
½ cup white vinegar
1½ teaspoons salt
2 teaspoons powdered garlic
2 teaspoons powdered onion
²⁄₃ cup salad oil
¼ cup honey

Combine all ingredients in blender or food processor and whip together until well blended, at least one minute. Yield: Approximately 5½ cups.

Raspberry Vinaigrette

1 cup salad oil
½ cup olive oil
¾ cup white vinegar
¾ cup honey
1 teaspoon fresh ground pepper
2 cups frozen whole raspberries
¼ teaspoon salt

Mix all ingredients in large mixing bowl of electric mixer and stir together well on low to medium speed until smooth. Do not whip at high speed. Mixing should be for approximately 3 minutes. Yield: 5 cups.

French Dressing

2 cups ketchup
1 egg
1 cup salad oil
½ cup wine vinegar
2½ tablespoons Dijon mustard
1½ tablespoons Worcestershire sauce
1 tablespoon tarragon
1½ tablespoons lemon juice
salt and pepper to taste

Combine all ingredients in blender or food processor and whip together until well blended. (Approximately one minute). Yield: Approximately 1 quart (4 cups).

Bleu Cheese Dressing

2 cups sour cream
¾ cup buttermilk
½ pound crumbled Bleu cheese

Mix very slowly in food processor, or at medium speed with an electric mixer, until well blended but pieces of bleu cheese remain visible. Yield: Approximately one quart (4 cups).

Thousand Island Dressing

½ cup ketchup
4 cups mayonnaise
2 tablespoons Worcestershire sauce
⅓ cup onion, minced
½ cup green pepper, chopped
¾ cup salad olives, chopped (small stuffed green olives)
2 eggs, hard-boiled and chopped
⅛ teaspoon red pepper, dry ground
1½ teaspoons brown sugar
1½ teaspoons cider vinegar

Blend all ingredients together in electric mixer at low speed. Then blend at high speed for one minute. Yield: Approximately 1½ quarts.

Italian Dressing

1⅓ *cups olive oil*
1⅓ *cups salad oil*
1⅓ *cups cider vinegar*
1 *tablespoon leaf oregano*
1 *tablespoon sweet basil*
1 *tablespoon sugar*
1 *teaspoon pepper, fresh ground*
1 *tablespoon garlic, freshly chopped*

Stir all ingredients together with wire whisk. Shake before using. Yield: One quart.

French Vinaigrette

1 *cup red wine vinegar*
3 *cups salad oil*
6 *tablespoons sugar*
1 *tablespoon paprika*
1 *tablespoon salt*
3 *garlic cloves, crushed*

Stir all ingredients together with wire whisk. Shake before using. Yield: 5 cups.

The White Gull Inn

Est. 1896

Side Dishes

Notes

Candlelight Dinner Rice Pilaf

½ medium chopped onion
1 stalk chopped celery
½ cup sliced mushrooms
¼ medium chopped green pepper
1½ cups uncooked white rice
1 cup uncooked wild rice
4 cups chicken stock
½ teaspoon marjoram
½ teaspoon tarragon
½ teaspoon thyme
½ teaspoon salt

Saute all vegetables and wild rice together until onions are transparent. Add white rice, chicken stock, and spices, and blend well while simmering. Continue to simmer covered on stove over low heat for another 30 minutes. Makes 6 to 8 servings.

Side Dishes

Corn and Clam Pie

¼ cup butter
1 onion, chopped
1 cup celery, chopped
¼ cup flour
½ teaspoon salt
¼ teaspoon pepper
¼ teaspoon thyme leaves
1 6½-ounce can minced clams, with juice
1 cup milk
1 cup frozen whole kernel corn

Preheat oven to 400 degrees. Heat butter in large saucepan. Add onions and celery and saute 10 minutes. Stir in flour, salt, pepper, and thyme until well combined. Gradually add clams and juice, milk and corn. Bring to a boil, stirring constantly. Reduce heat and simmer, stirring occasionally, for 10 minutes. Fill pie shell and cover with top crust. Brush top of pie before baking with a mixture of egg yolk and water for a shiny crust. Bake at 350 degrees for about 30 minutes or until golden brown.

Early American Buffet Baked Beans

1 medium chopped onion
1 pound great northern beans
¼ cup brown sugar
½ cup chopped bacon, uncooked
1 teaspoon salt
½ teaspoon black pepper
⅓ cup molasses
3 tablespoons ketchup
water

Place beans in a large bowl. Add enough water to cover the beans, and soak overnight (6-8 hours). Mix beans with other ingredients. Cook on low setting of crock pot, or covered in a conventional oven at 225 degrees for 3 to 4 hours, until the beans become a rich brown color, and all moisture is absorbed. Yield: 8 cups.

The Door County Fish Boil

It is dusk in Fish Creek, and a gusty wind whips a few leaves about the patio. The dinner guests at the White Gull Inn don't seem to mind the falling temperatures. They are all outside, standing around a huge black pot, filled with boiling water and suspended over a blazing wood fire. Clutching mugs of beer and cider, they huddle close to the flames, keeping warm and straining to hear the tall man who appears to be skimming the pot and giving a short course in cooking.

Some of the guests are locals entertaining out of town visitors. The rest are tourists, experiencing something everyone has heard about from the moment they set foot on the Door Peninsula—a traditional outdoor fish boil. And the cook at center stage is Russ Ostrand, dean of the Door County "master boilers."

"I'm half German," says Russ, slowly measuring his words, in answer to a question. "Half Danish and half Swedish. Thay's why I'm so big—three halves." The group laughs, and the questioner knows he's been had, but doesn't mind. It's part of the fun of attending a fish boil: meeting Russ, hearing the history, learning the procedure and tasting fish prepared in a way few people have outside of Door County. In case that's not enough, in between cooking and explaining, Russ picks up his antique button accordian and conjures up German and other European folk tunes.

No doubt the freshly caught Lake Michigan whitefish, the outdoor wood fire and the 100-year-old inn all contribute to the fish boil's appeal. But few would dispute that the main ingredient in this unique event is Russ, a Door County native who has been performing this ritual much of his life, and for the last 25 years at the White Gull.

Born and raised on a farm in West Jacksonport, Russ taught himself how to play accordian more than fifty years ago on a model he bought out of a Sears catalog for $8.94, money he had earned picking cherries. Over the years, while Russ supported his family as a "shipyard farmer"—a pipe fitter at Peterson's who farmed eighty acres in his spare time—he moonlighted with his accordian at weddings and other community events. In 1965, one of those moonlighting

69

jobs led to his signing on at the White Gull as resident musician at the fish boils. As a native, Russ had boiled fish before, so soon he took over that job too.

"How did the fish boil get started?" asks another guest. Russ patiently begins the answer as though he has never heard the question before. "Well, people have been boiling fish for thousands of years. I don't know who did it first in Door County. Maybe the commercial fishermen who had access to lots of fish, and wanted a quick and easy meal. I first remember it when churches did it to raise money when I was growing up. People came from all around to taste the local fish, potatoes, and Door County cherry pie. I just figured they boiled it because how else would you cook fish for such a large group?

"Back in the 1950s, when Peterson's would have a picnic for the yard, it was usually a fish boil. I was always asked to bring my accordian and play. After a while, I'd been to so many that I just knew how to boil fish.

"Eventually (about 1959) the restaurants figured that tourists might like fish boils too." And then, with his characteristic understatement, "And I think they may have been right."

Russ is now adding the salt, something which never fails to catch the crowd's attention because of the amount used in the fish boil recipe—one pound for every two gallons of water. "Is that salt?" someone gasps. "Just a pinch," answers Russ. Then, with a smile forming on his face, red from the heat, he explains. "The salt does not make the fish and potatoes salty. It raises the specific gravity of the water. Kind of makes it like the ocean and everything wants to float. All the fish oils that we don't want to eat rise to the surface. When the fish and potatoes are done (the potatoes, after 30 minutes of boiling, the fish being added for the last nine minutes) I throw on a small amount of kerosene."

At this point, invariably, someone asks if the kerosene goes into the pot itself. Knowing that boiled fish doesn't sound too appealing to begin with—until you've tried it—Russ stresses that the kerosene goes on the fire only. The big flareup, he explains, causes the overboil, when the water in the top half of the pot boils over the edge, and takes the oil with it.

That "small amount of kerosene" is now being measured into an old coffee can by Russ's assistant. You can tell those who've been here before because they move back, forming a wide ring around the fire and the boiler. For the newcomers, Russ warns, "Better give it plenty of room. If the wind shifts, it's likely to shorten your hair." With the crowd at a respectful distance and his assistant behind him, ready with a long pole, Russ tosses the kerosene on the

flames. A wall of fire shoots skyward, and water pours over the side of the pot, hissing as it hits the coals. A dozen camera flashes go off, as the assistant and Russ ease the pole through the nets of fish and potatoes, lifting them gently out to set on a nearby tray.

Russ now pauses and peers into the net for a moment, as if to see if the fish is properly cooked. That it wouldn't be is hard to fathom, since Russ by now has cooked nearly half a million servings. Finally, he raises his head and says incredulously to his assistant, just loud enough for those around them to hear, "It looks good enough to eat!"

Inside the dining room, the dinner guests devour the fish and potatoes, doused in melted butter and served with the traditional accompaniments of coleslaw, rye bread and cherry pie. And plenty of Wisconsin beer—usually Special Export—for that's what the boiler himself is drinking, as he readies himself with his accordian. The first tune is a toe-tapper like "My Favorite Polka," something to get everyone in the mood. Later will come the sing-a-longs like "Let Me Call You Sweetheart" and "When Irish Eyes Are Smiling." Requests are popular, like the "Anniversary Waltz." Perhaps it's some lucky soul's birthday, and when a waitress appears from the kitchen with a candle sticking out of a piece of pie, the accordian leads eighty voices in a rousing "Happy Birthday." Once in a while, depending on the crowd, the mood and the amount of Export consumed, a couple will get up and begin to polka, egged on by much hand-clapping from the rest of the dining room.

Finally, the music stops, Russ stands up, puts down his accordian and heads outside, where another group is gathering. As he pours five pounds of salt into the pot, someone asks, "Is that salt?" For a moment, Russ feigns a worried look. "I hope so," he says soberly. Then, with a smile, he starts all over.

Russ sold the farm in 1977. Seven of his eight kids were grown, and he and his wife, Irene, decided to move to a smaller, new home in Sturgeon Bay. He retired from his job as head of the pipe fitting department at Peterson's in 1983. He's kept busy since by buying older homes called "handyman specials," fixing them up himself and reselling them.

And he is still boiling. Four nights a week all summer long and one or two nights in winter. On the hottest dog days of July and in subzero, wind-chilled nights of early January. People who watched Russ cook their first fish boil from the shoulders of a parent in the sixties now bring their little ones, wondering if he's still here. They aren't disappointed. You can set your clock by the way Russ rounds the corner of the dining room on fish boil nights, accordian in hand,

exactly 45 minutes before the first fish boil. Someone calls out, "How are you, Russ?"

"Normal," is his stock answer, and everyone smiles, as this sounds just as reassuring and funny as it did the first time he said it.

Another group that returns to see Russ often are those who, as high school and college students, worked their first job alongside him at the fish boils. They never quite forget the kind man with the gentle sense of humor, who approaches each day, each new boil, each new or returning face as a challenge—worthy of his best effort. And Russ is fond of the young (and now not so young) people he's worked with through the years, remembering most of their names. They like to reminisce and stimulate old memories, some good, some outrageous.

Like the time in '72 when the serving table collapsed and the lemon bread spilled all over the floor, covered with tartar sauce. You could hear a pin drop until Russ broke the silence with, "Anyone know any good jokes?" Everyone cracked up and Russ broke into a tune on his accordian while the staff righted the table and brought out fresh food.

And the time there was a bat in the lobby, and fifty people hit the deck. Or when Glen, the assistant boiler back in '76, dropped a whole net of cooked fish on the patio. It wouldn't have been so bad, but there wasn't enough fish left in the cooler to feed the crowd. Russ calmly boiled what was on hand and sent Glen down the street to borrow fish from a competitor. By the time the first batch was cooked, Glen had made it back with just enough for the rest, and the show went on.

And there was the time, after Russ warned everyone to stand back for the overboil, he turned quickly to avoid the flames and knocked over one of the owners' wives. "It kind of was real bad," says Russ, "because she had a cast on at the time that ran all the way up her leg. But I had told everyone to stand back." What did she do then? "Oh, she wasn't hurt," he says. "She and I had a good laugh."

And remember the time, back in the days when people used to eat out on the patio in summer, when that line squall moved through? Everyone grabbed their food and dashed for cover, as the staff went through its storm drill of moving tables and chairs. After everyone was situated, a staff member looked out the window to discover that someone had forgotten a baby out in the rain. Nowadays, that couldn't happen, as everyone eats inside, rain or shine. The only two people that have to be outside are Russ and his assistant. People ask

Russ, "What do you do when it rains?" to which he answers, "I get wet."

Fish boils are newsworthy, because Door County is the only place that has them. And people like Russ are newsworthy because other places don't have him, either. Russ has had his fair share of publicity, and has had his picture in "Better Homes & Gardens," "Country Living," and "The New York Times." In 1987, when Milwaukee's Channel 4 wanted to do a live broadcast from Door County, they parked their satellite dish out on Main Street in Fish Creek, just so their anchor could interview Russ live. Russ is always gracious in these interviews, but it doesn't change the way he is. He likes working, he enjoys playing the accordian, and he likes people.

And he loves whitefish. Every night before leaving, right before he plays "Goodnight, Irene," Russ has a big helping of it in the kitchen. "In the beginning, I got a little sick of it, eating it four nights a week," he recalls. "By the end of summer, I might only have it once or twice a week. But then, after a few years, I began to like it all the time again. In fact, when I'm not boiling regularly, I kind of miss it."

Compared with Russ, I'm a relative newcomer to the fish boil business, having worked with him since 1972. In the early years I worked alongside him a lot more, as his assistant. In recent years I've filled in for him on the few occasions when he is absent. I know I miss him when he's not there, and I suspect that others do too. For when I'm his substitute, and I walk into work and strap on my apron, the first thing each staff member and each customer says to me is, "Hi, where's Russ?"

White Gull Inn
Fish Boil

12 small red potatoes
8 quarts water
2 cups salt
12 whitefish steaks, cut two inches thick
melted butter
lemon wedges

EQUIPMENT NEEDED:

5 gallon pot.
Removable basket for pot, or 2-24"x24" pieces of
cheesecloth, or collander.

73

At the White Gull Inn, we cook the fish outside over a wood fire, using a 22-gallon pot and two nets, one for the fish and one for the potatoes. This recipe is for cooking at home on your kitchen stove. You will need a large (5 gallon is ideal) pot, preferably with a removable basket or net, for draining. For smaller quantities, one basket or net is sufficient for both the potatoes and fish. If your pot does not have a removable basket for draining, you can make one cheese-cloth bag to hold the potatoes and one to hold the fish, or drain the food in the sink, using a collander.

Wash potatoes and cut a small slice from each end, for flavor penetration. Bring the water in the pot to a boil; keep it boiling as much as possible throughout the cooking procedure.

Add the potatoes and one half the salt; cook 20 minutes. Check doneness of potatoes with a fork; they should be almost done. When potatoes are almost done, add whitefish with the remaining salt. Cook approximately 8-10 minutes, until fish are still firm, but begin to pull away from the bone when lifted with a fork. At the inn, when cooking outside, we toss a small amount of kerosene on the fire when the fish is done, causing the fish oils, which have risen to the surface of the water, to boil over the sides. Do not attempt this at home; simply skim the oils off the surface with a spoon while the fish is cooking.

Lift cooked potatoes and fish from the water; drain. Serve immediately with melted butter and lemon. Yield: Four generous servings.

(Traditional fish boil accompaniments are coleslaw, homemade limpa bread, lemon, orange date nut, and pumpkin bread, and Door County cherry pie for dessert.)

The amount of salt used in the fish boil is based on the amount of water. To expand this recipe, add 1 cup salt for each additional gallon of water.

The White Gull Inn

Est. 1896

Entrees

Notes

Seafood Stir Fry

1 cup shrimp, medium-sized
1 cup langustinos, or lobster, or crab, or clams
1 cup diced green onions
1 cup diced carrots
1 cup diced broccoli hearts or water chestnuts
1 cup diced celery
½ cup pea pods
1 cup sliced mushrooms
2 tablespoons butter

SAUCE:
4 tablespoons butter
4 tablespoons flour
1 cup fish stock, or substitute 1 tablespoon seafood base
   to 1 cup water
¼ teaspoon powdered ginger
¼ teaspoon white pepper
½ teaspoon salt
¼ teaspoon cayenne pepper
1 tablespoon soy sauce
½ teaspoon garlic
1 cup heavy cream

Saute all vegetables in butter for 2 minutes. Add shrimp, saute 1 minute longer. Add other chosen seafood and enough white sauce to cover stir fried ingredients lightly. Heat thoroughly, but do not boil. Serve over rice.

SAUCE: Melt butter in saucepan. Add flour slowly while stirring, to make roux. Simmer over low heat for 5 minutes. Do not allow to burn or darken. Add fish stock to roux. Simmer together while stirring frequently, until it becomes slightly thick. Add seasonings and soy sauce. Continue stirring and simmering 2 minutes more. Add cream just before pouring over vegetables, but do not allow to boil. Yield: Four 1½ cup servings.

Baked Whitefish with Apples and Mustard Sauce

2 whitefish fillets
1 large red tart apple, thinly wedged
¾ cup seafood stock (if unavailable, chicken stock)
½ cup white wine
¼ cup apple cider (for sauce) plus ⅛ cup for coating
5 teaspoons stone ground mustard (for sauce) plus 2 teaspoons
   for coating
2 teaspoons Dijon mustard
2 tablespoons butter
3 tablespoons flour
2 tablespoons heavy cream
salt and pepper to taste

Combine stock, wine, and cider, and bring to boil. Melt the butter, add flour and cook to form roux. With the stock mixture at a boil, gradually add roux whisking constantly, until the mixture coats a spoon heavily. Add 5 teaspoons stone ground mustard and 2 teaspoons Dijon mustard. Salt and pepper to taste. Whisk in heavy cream.

Spread the 2 teaspoons stone ground mustard on the fish fillets, top with apple slices and ⅛ cup cider, bake at 350 degrees until done (usually 5-7 minutes for a Lake Michigan whitefish fillet) and top with sauce. Yield: Two servings.

Chicken Walnut

2 boneless, skinless chicken breasts, cut in halves
1 cup seasoned flour (see below)
2 tablespoons butter
2 teaspoons minced shallots
1 cup finely chopped walnuts (a food processor may be used)
1½ cup chicken broth
2 cups fresh spinach leaves
2 tablespoons balsamic vinegar
½ cup heavy cream

SEASONED FLOUR:
1 cup flour mixed together with 1 teaspoon salt, 1 teaspoon pepper,
*   1 teaspoon garlic powder, 2 teaspoons paprika*

Dredge breast fillets in the seasoned flour, then immediately saute in hot butter until browned on both sides, approximately 2 minutes on each side. Add shallots and walnuts and allow to brown slightly, approximately 30 seconds.

Add chicken broth and reduce heat. Simmer uncovered until sauce thickens and chicken is completely cooked, approximately 15 minutes.

Add cream and swirl the pan to combine the liquids and juices. Continue to simmer on low heat until thickened to desired consistency.

Dip the fresh spinach into the vinegar. Shake off excess. Arrange spinach into two servings onto dining plates, and serve the completed chicken with its sauce, over the spinach. Yield: 2 servings.

Entrees

Shrimp and Artichoke Romano

2 tablespoons clarified butter
8 jumbo shrimp
6 artichoke hearts, cut in half lengthwise
1 tablespoon minced garlic (or two small cloves)
½ cup dry white wine
6 tablespoons grated Romano cheese
4 tablespoons unsalted butter, at room temperature
¼ pound uncooked linguine
2 teaspoons fresh chopped parsley

Cook linguine al dente and drain well. Set aside. Saute shrimp and artichoke hearts in the clarified butter for 2 to 3 minutes or until the shrimp is almost completely done. Add garlic and cook with salt and pepper until garlic browns just slightly, approximately 20 seconds. Add white wine and cheese and simmer over medium heat until the liquid is slightly thickened, approximately 30 seconds. Reduce heat and add unsalted butter one tablespoon at a time, incorporating it into the sauce by using a swirling motion with the pan. Be careful not to allow the sauce to boil. When done, the sauce will be the consistency of heavy cream. Toss in cooked linguine, swirl together to heat and distribute evenly, and serve immediately. Garnish with the chopped parsley. Yield: 2 servings.

Seafood Pot Pie

1 cup raw clams
1 cup peeled deveined shrimp
1 cup deboned chunked haddock
4 stalks celery
1 large onion, chunked
2 large carrots, chunked
3 large potatoes, cubed
3½ cups water
2 tablespoons fish soup base or seafood boullion
1½ teaspoons white pepper
1 teaspoon salt
3 bay leaves
2 teaspoons thyme
2 tablespoons butter
prepared puff pastry (approximately 10"x16" inch piece)

Saute onions, celery, and carrots, until onions become transparent, in deep heavy saucepan. Add the soup base dissolved in the water. Add the spices and potato and simmer on medium heat until potatoes become just tender. Add seafood during the last 10 minutes of simmering. Remove bay leaves. Divide filling equally between 6 individual casserole dishes. Cut prepared puff pastry into circles slightly larger in circumference than the top of the casseroles. Lay each circle of pastry over the filled dish and press lightly around the rim to seal. Vent holes are not necessary, but if 'drawn' with a knife, designs become very attractive during baking. For a glossy finish, brush ½ cup water and 1 egg, well beaten, over top of crust, very lightly, before baking. Bake at 400 degrees for approximately 20 minutes, or until golden brown. Yield: Six 1½ cup servings.

Beef Stew

2½ pounds beef stew meat, cubed
½ bunch celery, chunked
1 large onion, chunked
1½ pounds carrots, chunked
5½ cups water
3 tablespoons beef soup base or bouillon
½ cup Kitchen Bouquet
1 teaspoon black pepper
2 bay leaves
1 teaspoon thyme
2 pounds potatoes, peeled and cubed

Brown meat in lightly oiled or buttered deep heavy saucepan. Add vegetables, water and seasoning, and simmer for 30 minutes. Add potatoes and simmer another 30 minutes, or until potatoes are tender. Thicken with roux at this point.

ROUX: Melt ½ cup butter or margarine in frypan, then slowly stir in ½ cup flour with wire whisk or fork until blended smoothly. Cook over medium heat for one minute.

Add roux in ¼ cup portions to vegetable and beef mixture until stew reaches desired thickness, allowing stew to simmer 2 minutes between each added portion of roux. Simmer on low heat at least another 30 minutes before serving. Yield: 4 quarts.

Beef Wellington

3 cups mushrooms
3 cloves fresh chopped garlic
4 fresh chopped shallots
2 tablespoons butter
4 6-ounce tenderloins
puff pastry (4, 9"x12" inch pieces)

Saute first four ingredients until moisture has been cooked out of mushrooms. Puree in blender to a thick paste. By following the diagrams below, place each tenderloin on a piece of puff pastry, top each with one quarter of puree, and fold pastry up and around the steak according to the sketches. For a glossy finish to the pastry, brush top of completed Wellington lightly with a mixture of ½ cup water, and 1 egg, well beaten, just prior to baking. Bake at 400 degrees until desired degree of doneness is achieved. 40 to 45 minutes will yield medium rare, 50 minutes medium, 55 to 60 minutes medium well. A meat thermometer may also be used to determine doneness. Yield: 4 servings.

A

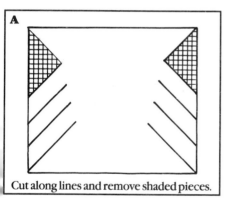

Cut along lines and remove shaded pieces.

B

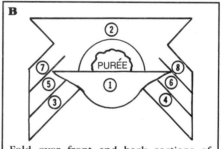

Fold over front and back sections of pastry and mold gently around tenderloin with hands.

C

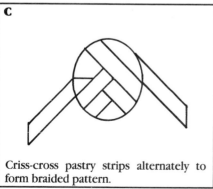

Criss-cross pastry strips alternately to form braided pattern.

D

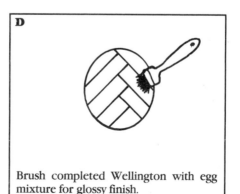

Brush completed Wellington with egg mixture for glossy finish.

Entrees

Whitefish with Hazelnut Butter

6 ounces unsalted butter at room temperature
4 ounces roasted, peeled, and chopped hazelnuts
2 teaspoons fresh chopped parsley
2 teaspoons minced shallots
pinch of salt
pinch of cayenne pepper
2 whitefish fillets

Prepare whitefish by sprinkling with salt and pepper and dot with butter. Blend the 6 ounces of unsalted butter, hazelnuts, parsley, shallots, and cayenne on medium speed of blender for 30 seconds.

Broil the fillets for 7 minutes, or until just about done. Remove from broiler and spread with hazelnut butter. Finish cooking by returning to broiler for another 1½ minutes. Yield: Serves 2.

Stuffed Cornish Game Hens with Cherry Glaze

4 cornish game hens
3 medium red apples
4 cups frozen red tart cherries in juice (thawed)
½ cup sugar
2 tablespoons cornstarch

Rinse hens and trim out excess fat from cavity. Dice apples and mix with 2 cups of drained cherries (reserving liquid). Stuff hens with fruit mixture. Bake covered for one hour at 350 degrees and an additional 45 minutes at 375 degrees uncovered or until browned. Drain remaining cherries and add sugar and cornstarch to liquid. Cook until thickened. Add cherries and spoon over hens when serving. Serve remaining sauce on the side. Yield: 4 servings.

Entrees

The White Gull Inn

Est. 1896

Desserts

Notes

Cherry Nut Bread Pudding

8 cups bread cubes
4 cups scalded milk
¼ pound butter, melted
1 cup sugar
4 eggs
½ teaspoon salt
1½ teaspoons cinnamon
½ teaspoon nutmeg
½ cup chopped nuts
2 tablespoons flour
4 cups red tart cherries, packed in own juice

Combine sugar, eggs, salt, cinnamon, and nutmeg in mixing bowl and beat until well blended at medium speed for 1-2 minutes. Set aside. Scald milk by bringing nearly to a boil then removing from heat. Melt butter by placing it into scalded milk. Set aside. Drain cherries from juice. Measure out 2⅔ cups cherries and toss them with the flour. Save the remaining cherries and juice for cherry sauce. Combine cooled milk and butter with the egg mixture. In greased 8"x8" pan, combine cherries, bread cubes, and chopped nuts. Pour milk and egg mixture over cube mixture in pan. Set pan into larger baking dish which has one inch of water in it. (This creates a steamy atmosphere in the oven). Bake 30-40 minutes at 350 degrees. Serve fresh from the oven with warmed cherry sauce. (See following page for CHERRY SAUCE). Yield: 6 servings.

Desserts

Cherry Sauce

(for preceding Cherry Nut Bread Pudding or ice cream sundaes!)

*1¹/₃ cups red tart cherries in their own juice (this is what will be
    remaining from the total cherries called for in the preceding
    recipe)*
1 tablespoon cornstarch
sugar (optional)

Pour cherry juice into medium saucepan and bring almost to a boil. If cherry juice is unsweetened, sweeten to taste at this point. Add desired sugar and stir until thoroughly dissolved. While continuously stirring with wire whisk, sprinkle cornstarch into cherry sauce slowly until smoothly blended and free of lumps. Allow to nearly return to boil and cook for one minute, stirring constantly and return whole cherries to the sauce. Remove from heat and set aside. Serve immediately over Cherry Nut Bread Pudding, or allow to cool before serving over ice cream. Yield: 1½ cups.

Poppy Seed Torte

¹/₃ cup poppy seeds
1½ teaspoons vanilla extract
¾ cup milk
¾ cup butter
1½ cups sugar
1¾ cups flour
2½ teaspoons baking powder
1 teaspoon salt
5 egg whites, stiffly beaten

FILLING:

½ cup sugar
1 tablespoon cornstarch
1½ cups milk
5 egg yolks
1 teaspoon vanilla extract
¼ cup chopped nuts (optional)

FROSTING:

1-1½ cups sugar (to taste)
1 pint whipping cream

Soak poppy seeds in milk for one hour. Whip egg whites until stiff, set aside. Add vanilla to seeds. Cream together butter and sugar in mixing bowl. Sift together flour, baking powder, and salt in another bowl. Add dry ingredients to the butter and sugar mixture. Mix in poppy seeds and liquid. Fold in egg whites.

Bake in two well greased 9″ round cake pans for 20 to 25 minutes at 375 degrees. Cool 10 minutes and remove from pans, then allow to cool completely. Prepare filling and refrigerate while cakes are baking.

FILLING: Combine sugar and cornstarch. Add milk and beaten egg yolks. Cook and stir continuously until bubbling, then cook one minute longer. Add vanilla and chopped nuts. Cover with plastic wrap and refrigerate until needed.

Split the cake layers in half horizontally. Spread ⅓ of the filling between each of the layers. Frost overall, top and sides, with whipped fresh cream which has been sweetened with sugar to taste.

Garnish cake with decoratively piped whipped cream, fresh lemon slices, or a sprinkling of poppy seeds.

Desserts

Bourbon Bread Pudding

1 pound bread cubes (approximately one loaf)
1 quart milk
3 eggs
1 cup sugar
2 tablespoons vanilla
1 cup raisins

BOURBON SAUCE:
2 eggs
1 cup sugar
1 cup butter
½ cup bourbon

Cut bread into medium sized cubes (approximately ½"x½") and allow to soak in milk, occasionally turning cubes gently. In another bowl beat sugar, eggs, and vanilla until well mixed. Add egg mixture to the bread cube mixture. Add raisins and turn gently again. Pour into well greased 8"x8" cake pan. Bake at 300 degrees for 1½ hours, covering the pan with aluminum foil after one hour.

BOURBON SAUCE: Whip eggs and sugar on high speed of electric mixer until it becomes a light lemon color. Add the 1 cup butter (melted) and bourbon to the egg mixture and blend on medium speed of electric mixer until very smooth, and sugar is completely dissolved. Serve bread pudding warm from the oven with the warmed bourbon sauce spooned over each serving, and garnish with whipped cream dollop if desired. Makes approximately 12 servings.

Apple or Cherry Crisp

8 cups chopped, peeled apples, or fresh or frozen cherries (drained)
½ cup flour (for fruit)
¾ cup flour (for topping)
2 cups rolled oats or unbaked granola (see page 24)
1½ cups brown sugar
2 teaspoons cinnamon
½ cup butter

Fill 9"x13" pan with cherries or apples which have been tossed with the ½ cup of flour. Mix the rest of the dry ingredients and moisten with melted butter until mixture forms crumbs. Sprinkle over fruit. Bake 30 to 35 minutes at 350 degrees. Remove from oven and let set for 30 minutes. Then serve still warm with your favorite ice cream. Yield: 8 to 10 servings.

Peanut Butter Cream Pie with Hot Fudge

4 eggs
1½ cups sugar
½ cup creamy type peanut butter
1 cup butter at room temperature
2 teaspoons vanilla
1 cup chopped peanuts
1 cup hot fudge sauce from recipe found on page 94
whipped cream

GRAHAM CRACKER CRUST:
1 cup graham cracker crumbs
½ cup sugar
¼ cup butter

Combine sugar, peanut butter, butter, and vanilla. Mix well. Add one egg and beat 5 minutes. Repeat this one egg at a time and beating 5 minutes between each until all eggs are added. Pour mixture into pie crust and top with ¾ of the chopped peanuts. Chill thoroughly until firm, approximately 1 hour. To serve, spoon heated hot fudge by the heaping tablespoon over each individual slice, top with a dollop of whipped cream if desired, and sprinkle remaining chopped peanuts over pie.

GRAHAM CRACKER CRUST: Blend dry ingredients. Cut butter into graham cracker mixture and line into a 9″ deep dish pie plate.

Hot Fudge

1 ounce powdered baker's cocoa
¼ cup hot water
¾ cup sweetened condensed milk
¾ cup corn syrup
½ teaspoon salt
¼ cup melted butter
¾ teaspoon vanilla
¼ teaspoon cinnamon
10 ounces bittersweet chocolate (melted)

In small bowl, stir cocoa and water together until smooth. In food processor, or high speed of traditional mixer, combine remaining ingredients. Add dissolved cocoa and blend for at least one full minute until very smooth texture is achieved. Yield: 3 cups.

Lemon Mousse

¾ cup sugar
1 envelope unflavored gelatin
2 teaspoons finely shredded lemon peel
1½ teaspoons cornstarch
1 cup lemon juice
4 beaten egg yolks
1½ cups whipping cream
2 tablespoons orange liqueur
6 stiffly beaten egg whites

In a 1½ quart saucepan, combine sugar, gelatin, lemon peel, and cornstarch. Stir in lemon juice and egg yolks. Cook and stir till thickened and bubbly. Cook and stir 2 minutes more. Remove from heat; cover the surface with clear plastic wrap. Chill thoroughly.

Whip cream to soft peaks. Turn chilled lemon mixture into a blender container or food processor bowl; add orange liqueur. Cover; blend till smooth. Pour mixture into large mixing bowl; fold in whipped cream, then the stiff-beaten egg whites. Turn into a 2-quart serving bowl, or individual dessert (parfait or sherbet) glasses. Garnish with lemon slices. Makes 8 1-cup servings.

Chocolate Mousse

4 ounces semi-sweet chocolate
2 egg whites
¼ cup sugar
2 cups whipping cream

Melt chocolate in the microwave or over a double boiler. Cool till luke warm. Beat egg whites well. Combine chocolate and egg whites. Whip sugar and cream until very stiff. Fold very carefully to combine ingredients and spoon into dessert glasses. Chill thoroughly. Garnish with whipped cream and shaved chocolate. Makes 5 1-cup servings.

NOTE: If melting chocolate in microwave, use low setting, and stop to stir chocolate frequently.

Raisin Orange Cake

1 teaspoon baking soda
2 cups flour
1 cup sugar
½ cup shortening
2 eggs
1 cup sour milk
1 unpeeled orange, halved
1½ cups raisins

Squeeze most of the juice from orange halves, and set aside one half of the juice for later use in frosting. Grind remainder of orange in food processor or blender and set aside. Combine dry ingredients. Add shortening, eggs, and milk. Beat well. Stir in raisins and the ½ of orange juice allocated for the cake, and mix well.

Pour batter into 8"x8" inch well greased cake pan. Bake at 350 degrees until cake springs back from light touch to top, or toothpick or knife inserted comes out clean. Allow to completely cool before frosting.

FROSTING:
2 cups confectioner's sugar
1 teaspoon butter
½ juice of the above orange

Beat sugar and butter with mixer until well blended, then add orange juice and beat until very smooth. Spread over cooled cake.

Door County Cherry Pie

1½ cups sifted flour
¾ teaspoon salt
½ cup lard
4 tablespoons ice water
5 cups fresh red tart cherries, pitted

EITHER:
2 teaspoons Kirsch
or
2 drops almond extract
1 teaspoon grated lemon rind
1 cup sugar
⅛ teaspoon salt
4 tablespoons flour
1 tablespoon butter

Cut half of lard into flour and salt with a pastry blender to obtain a coarse meal consistency. Add remaining lard and cut again with pastry blender. Sprinkle dough with water, mixing lightly with a fork until it just holds together. Chill. Line a 9″ pie pan with pastry, saving ⅓ of the dough for the lattice top crust. In separate mixing bowl, mix cherries, the flavoring of your choice, (kirsch or almond extract), and lemon rind together. Combine sugar, salt and flour. Add cherries and mix well. Pour filling into lined pie pan. Dot with butter and cover with lattice work crust.

Bake at 450 degrees for 10 minutes then reduce heat to 350 and bake 30 minutes longer or until golden brown.

Cranberry Apple Pie

1 9-inch pie shell (bottom crust only)
1 12-ounce bag of cranberries
5 apples, peeled, cored, chopped
1 cup sugar
4 tablespoons cornstarch
1 teaspoon cinnamon
½ teaspoon nutmeg
1 teaspoon orange peel, finely grated

TOPPING:
1 cup flour
⅓ cup brown sugar
⅓ cup sugar
1 teaspoon cinnamon
⅓ cup butter

Combine dry ingredients and seasoning. Toss with prepared apples and cranberries. Pour into unbaked pie shell and bake without streusel topping for 30 minutes at 350 degrees.

TOPPING: Combine dry ingredients. Cut butter into dry ingredients until mixture is coarse and crumb-like. Sprinkle topping over partially baked pie.

Bake completely assembled pie at 350 degrees for another 30 minutes or until crumb topping appears golden brown.

The White Gull Today

Staying at the White Gull Inn today is like traveling back to the turn of the century—but bringing along modern comforts. While the facades of the buildings remain unchanged and many of the original furnishings accent the rooms, much work has been done in recent years. Since 1972, every building has received a new roof and foundation, new wiring and been insulated for winter use.

As in many other older inns, the White Gull rooms run the gamut from cozy, original rooms with shared baths to elegant, spacious rooms with private bathrooms and fireplaces. Founders Herman and Henriette Welcker prided themselves on their good taste in furniture, and the walnut, oak or iron beds guests sleep in are likely to be one of the Welckers' acquisitions. Over the years, many other antiques have been added, and the rooms are decorated with coordinating prints and fabrics that maintain the warm, turn of the century flavor. Comfort, however, is strictly up-to-date, with firm mattresses, air conditioning, modern plumbing and little touches that make guests as comfortable as can be.

On the first floor of the main lodge, guests have a choice of three rooms, all with private entrance, and one of which has a fireplace. Upstairs, the rooms are smaller, but all open onto wicker-filled verandas. The four rooms in Cliffhouse and the one-bedroom Henriette Cottage, behind the main lodge, are popular for honeymoons and other special occasions because of their elegant furnishings and fireplaces. Families and couples traveling together enjoy the three-bedroom Stowaway and Beachcomber Cottages and four-bedroom Lundberg House, all of which have fireplaces.

Breakfast at the White Gull means waking up to the smell of fresh ground coffee and coffeecake arising from the kitchen. Late sleepers appreciate that the Eggs Benedict, White Gull granola, hash browns, and buttermilk pancakes with real Door County maple syrup are served until noon. Lunches include hearty homemade soups, sandwiches, omelets, salads, and tempting desserts from the White Gull bakery.

Entrees at the quiet, candlelit dinners feature fresh "catch-of-the-day" whitefish, roasted Wisconsin duckling and other regional specialties. Only the freshest of produce and ingredients are used, and each meal is thoughtfully prepared to order. The White Gull Inn traditional fish boil is served Wednesday, Friday, Saturday, and Sunday evenings in summer and fall, and on Wednesday and Saturday nights the rest of the year.

Door County Seasons

Originally, the White Gull Inn and most of the businesses in Door County were only open between Memorial Day and Labor Day. This is still a popular time, for there is nearly every imaginable recreational activity, from golf to wind surfing, from hiking and biking to sailing and charter fishing. Door County's five state parks offer miles of trails to explore, and art galleries can be found in every nook and cranny. The Peninsula Players, America's oldest professional summer stock theatre, performs in Fish Creek, as does the renowned Peninsula Music Festival.

For a long time, Door County autumns were a well kept secret. However, in recent years, people from all over the midwest have begun making annual trips to the peninsula in September and October to witness what one writer described as the "caviar of fall color."

Winter is the peninsula's "Quiet Season," when the cedars and bluffs wear a mantle of white. The only "crowds" one is likely to encounter are deer. Guests spend their days exploring the miles of cross-country ski trails in Peninsula State Park, ice skating, snow shoeing or taking a sleigh ride from the front door of the inn. Evenings are spent before crackling fireplaces in guest rooms or the White Gull lobby.

The first sign of spring is the annual tapping of the sugar maple trees in early March, when days are sunny and warm, and temperatures fall below freezing at night. April is most popular with sport fishermen, who descend on each harbor as the ice goes out. May is a month of greening and rejuvenation, peaking with the bursting of blossoms in the many Door County cherry and apple orchards.

To accommodate the increasing number of guests who like to visit Door County in every season, The White Gull Inn is now open every day of the year except Thanksgiving and Christmas Day.

Index